THE HISTORY OF EXPLORATION
COLUMBUS
& THE RENAISSANCE EXPLORERS

NEW
FOREST
PRESS

Publisher: Tim Cook
Editor: Guy Croton
Designer: Carol Davis
Production Controller: Ed Green
Production Manager: Suzy Kelly

ISBN: 978-1-84898-305-2
Library of Congress Control Number: 2010925458
Tracking number: nfp0003

U.S. publication © 2010 New Forest Press
Published in arrangement with Black Rabbit Books

PO Box 784, Mankato, MN 56002
www.newforestpress.com

Printed in the USA
9 8 7 6 5 4 3 2 1

0298

Every effort has been made to trace the copyright holders, and we apologize in advance for any omissions.
We would be pleased to insert the appropriate acknowledgments in any subsequent edition of this publication.

CONTENTS

Greenland

NORTH AMERICA

Atlantic Ocean

From Lisbon

From Lisbon

From Lisbon

SOUTH AMERICA

KEY

1	*Columbus 1st Voyage*	
2	*Columbus 2nd Voyage*	
3	*Columbus 3rd Voyage*	
4	*Columbus 4th Voyage*	
5	*Cabot*	
6	*Frobisher*	
7	*Cartier*	
8	*Dias*	
9	*da Gama*	
10	*Cabral*	
11	*Willoughby*	
12	*Barents*	

THE VOYAGES OF COLUMBUS

INTRODUCTION

Exploration, that is the discovery of new lands, peoples, and cultures, has existed as long as mankind itself. It was however, during the "Age of Discovery" between the 15th and 17th centuries that exploration and discovery became increasingly important. It was the need for power and trade, especially for spices and precious metals, that drove the European explorers to seek out new trading partners, and lands to colonize. Along with improvements in shipbuilding, map reading, and navigation, this was a time of great change in the European view of the world.

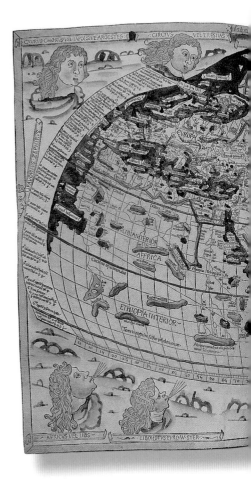

Since the ancient Greeks, man had believed that the Earth was at the center of the Universe, with the Sun, Moon, and stars rotating around it. This was known as the Ptolemaic (or geocentric) model. This theory remained popular until the late 16th century, when it was replaced by the Copernican (or heliocentric) model, championed by Nicolaus Copernicus and later Galileo, in which the planets rotate around the Sun.

CHRISTOPHER COLUMBUS

Christopher Columbus' intention was to find a westward route to China and the East Indies, as an eastward route was blocked by Muslim lands hostile to Europeans. Although Columbus was never to find Asia in his voyages, he did discover the continent of America after sailing across the Atlantic in 1492. He held the belief that it would be possible to continue sailing westward to reach Asia via America.

A VIEW OF THE WORLD

This map was first produced in 1482 and is called Ptolemy's world map. It shows how little of the world Europeans really knew about. Southern Africa, the Pacific, and the American continent are not included and Asia seems to be a matter of guesswork. Only the mapping of the Mediterranean is accurate. Even the outlines of Scotland and Ireland look strange to modern eyes.

FERDINAND MAGELLAN

Columbus' dream was to go on to inspire Ferdinand Magellan, whose voyages proved that, as Columbus believed, it was possible to reach Asia by traveling westward. Magellan traveled around South America, and across the Pacific, discovering the Strait of Magellan.

FRANCIS DRAKE

Francis Drake was to become the first Englishman to successfully circumnavigate the globe. He was commissioned by Elizabeth I to sail across the southern Atlantic through the Strait of Magellan and to attack the Spanish treasure ships and settlements on the unprotected west coast of South America.

THE MEDIEVAL VIEW OF THE WORLD

The people of medieval Europe had a very different view about the rest of the world than we do today. They did not have the benefit of newspapers, telephones, TV or the Internet, so news hardly ever reached ordinary people. Unlike today, they were not able to fly from one continent to another. In fact, very few people went farther than their nearest town during their entire lives. However, the way that medieval Europe looked at the world was to be changed forever by two explorers: Christopher Columbus, who sailed westward and found a new world in the Americas, and Vasco da Gama who sailed eastward and found a sea route to Asia.

THE MEDIEVAL CHURCH

The Christian people of medieval Europe were unified by a single religious belief. Everybody, from kings to peasants, was a member of the Roman Catholic Church. Although Catholics fought against each other, they all had a common hatred of non-Christians. The Roman Catholic Church believed that it had both a right and a duty to conquer and convert all nonbelievers.

THE CRUSADES

The Crusades started in 1095, when Pope Urban II urged all Christians to fight the Muslims and capture the holy city of Jerusalem. The First Crusade conquered Jerusalem in 1099, but the Muslims took it back soon afterward. There were six more unsuccessful Crusades between 1099 and 1250.

STORIES OF STRANGE CREATURES

Because many Europeans did not know about the people who lived in distant lands, there were many stories about strange and fantastic creatures who lived there. It was believed that there were people with the faces of dogs, people without heads and with their faces on their chests, and giants with only one eye in the middle of their forehead.

TRADE IN SPICES

Along with silk, the most important items traded between Asia and Europe were spices, such as nutmeg, shown here. Spices were important because medieval people had to eat meat that was either going rotten or had been preserved with salt. The spices helped disguise the putrid taste and extreme saltiness of the meat.

CHRISTOPHER COLUMBUS
-A TIMELINE-

~1441~

The first African slaves arrive in Portugal

~1445~

The Portuguese sail around Cape Verde, the western tip of West Africa

~c. 1451~

Christopher Columbus born in Genoa

~1460~

Prince Henry the Navigator dies

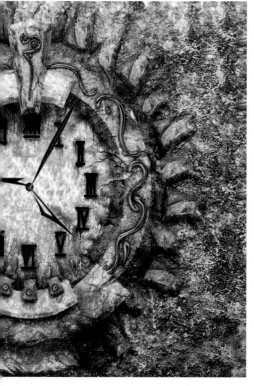

MEDIEVAL TIME

The medieval concept of time was very different from our own. The world turned much more slowly in those days—not literally, but in terms of the speed with which things happened. Although human lives were much shorter than now, everything took longer to happen and the way of life was generally very slow. A medieval person would be amazed by the incredible pace of the modern world.

SILK

The trade in silk between Asia and Europe was very important, but it was also very expensive. The silk had to come to Europe by land through Muslim traders, who controlled the trade between the two continents. Demand for silk among the wealthy was very high, creating huge profits for the traders.

MARCO POLO

Some Europeans had traveled long distances. Marco Polo set off for China in 1271 and arrived there more than three years later. He returned to Europe after 14 years, in 1295. His stories of China caught the imaginations of later explorers, although many people thought that some of his stories were untrue.

SIR JOHN MANDEVILLE

Some people wrote fictional travel stories full of wild exaggerations. In the 1350s, a book called *The Travels of Sir John Mandeville* appeared. It was this book that included many of the strange people that Europeans believed existed. One claimed that he met people with giant feet, which they used as a shelter from the Sun.

Columbus

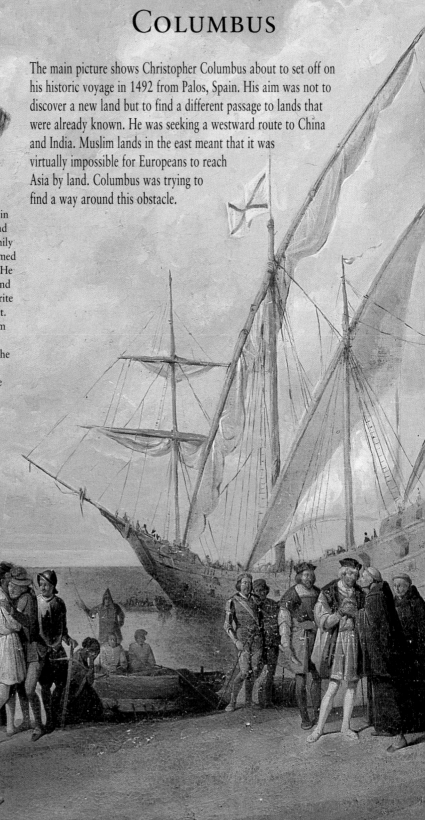

The main picture shows Christopher Columbus about to set off on his historic voyage in 1492 from Palos, Spain. His aim was not to discover a new land but to find a different passage to lands that were already known. He was seeking a westward route to China and India. Muslim lands in the east meant that it was virtually impossible for Europeans to reach Asia by land. Columbus was trying to find a way around this obstacle.

CHRISTOPHER COLUMBUS

Columbus was born in Genoa in Italy around 1451. Born into a family of weavers, he was named Cristoforo Colombo. He had little education and could not read and write until he was an adult. Like many boys from Genoa, he became a sailor. In 1476, at the age of 25, he was shipwrecked off the coast of Portugal.

EXPERIENCE IN SAILING

After his shipwreck, Columbus stayed on in Portugal and settled in Lisbon. He got married, learned to become a mapmaker, and continued his career as a sailor. He visited the west African coast, England, and Ireland. He later claimed that he also sailed to Iceland.

THE WEALTH OF THE INDIES

Columbus called his plan the "enterprise of the Indies." When medieval Europeans used the word "Indies," they did not mean just India, but also Japan, China, Indonesia, and Southeast Asia. It was believed that these were all very wealthy lands. Using Marco Polo's calculations, Columbus figured out that India was around 3,900 mi. (6,200km) west of Europe. In actual fact, this is more or less the distance between Europe and the American coast.

KING JOHN II OF PORTUGAL

It was while he was sailing in the Atlantic Ocean that Columbus deduced that it might be possible to sail westward from Europe to Asia. He first asked King John II of Portugal for help in 1484, but he was refused. The Portuguese were looking for a route to Asia around the African coast.

THE SPANISH INQUISITION

The Inquisition punished anybody who strayed from Roman Catholic teaching. They used torture in order to obtain confessions, and the guilty were often burned alive. In Spain, the Inquisition was used mostly against Jews, who were forced to convert to Christianity. Jews who refused to convert were ordered out of Spain on August 3, 1492, the day Columbus began his voyage across the Atlantic Ocean.

CHRISTOPHER COLUMBUS
-A TIMELINE-

~c. 1460~

Vasco da Gama born

~1476~

Columbus is shipwrecked off Portugal and starts to work for the Portuguese

~1482~

Diogo Cao sails farther along the west African coast than any other European

~1484~

King John II of Portugal turns down Columbus's request for help to sail westward

~1485~

Columbus moves to Spain to look for help from King Ferdinand and Queen Isabella

HERNANDO DE TALAVERA

The king and queen of Spain set up a special commission of priests, astrologers, and scholars to look at Columbus's proposals. This was headed by Hernando de Talavera, who was a monk and Queen Isabella's confessor. This church was named after him. The commission took until 1490 to come to a conclusion, and they advised the monarchs to reject Columbus's plan.

FERDINAND AND ISABELLA

Spain was divided into several kingdoms, the two largest being Castile and Aragon. The heir to the throne of Castile, Isabella, married the heir to the throne of Aragon, Ferdinand. When they both became the monarch of their own countries, the two thrones ruled together. A unified Spain, under Isabella I and Ferdinand II, was now much stronger.

SANTANGEL THE TREASURER

Columbus needed friends at the royal court to put his case to the king and queen. One of his major supporters was Santangel the Treasurer, who looked after the finances of the two monarchs. Without his support, Columbus's plan would have been rejected.

THE COURT OF
FERDINAND & ISABELLA

The refusal of King John II of Portugal to fund Columbus's plan to sail across the Atlantic Ocean to the Indies must have been a terrible blow to him. One year after John II had turned him down, Columbus decided to move with his family to Spain, to see if he could get support for his voyage there. A great deal of rivalry existed between Spain and Portugal, especially over finding a sea route to Asia. Columbus hoped to use this rivalry to convince the Spanish to support him and so have the advantage over the Portuguese. However, Columbus's plan to find a westward route to Asia seemed incredible to many people. Ferdinand and Isabella had to be convinced to finance a very risky venture.

THE NEED FOR GOLD

It was Ferdinand and Isabella's constant need for gold, even more than spices or silks, that made them finally accept Columbus's plan. The costs of waging war against the Moors and the expense of their magnificent court meant that they were very short of money.

THE RECONQUISTA

In the 700s, most of Spain was conquered by the Moors, Muslims from North Africa. The Spanish dreamed of driving them out and making Spain a Christian country again. Under Ferdinand and Isabella, the Reconquista (the "Reconquest") began, and by 1492, the Moors were finally pushed out of Spain, 700 years after they had first arrived.

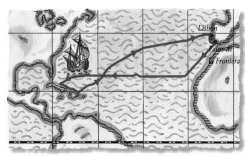

Columbus's 1st voyage ▬▬▬

Columbus's First Voyage

It took another two years for Ferdinand and Isabella to accept Talavera's recommendations and turn down Columbus's proposals. He was extremely disappointed. He was contemplating approaching the king of France when he met a new ally, a shipowner named Martin Alonso Pinzon. Columbus returned with his new partner and asked again for royal support. He also demanded that he be made governor of any new lands that he found and granted 10 percent of all the gold, jewels and spices. Ferdinand and Isabella refused him at first, but he gradually won them over. When he finally received royal approval, Columbus moved quickly. He and Pinzon soon had three ships ready to sail, and the journey began at dawn on August 3, 1492.

DEALING WITH MUTINY

Once the ships were out of sight of land, many of the sailors became nervous. They knew that they would reach land eventually, but they were afraid that they might run out of food before then and not be able to return to Spain. Columbus prevented the crew from mutinying and forced the ships to return to Spain by lying to them about how close they were to land.

LAND SIGHTED AT LAST

After several false alarms, land was finally sighted by a member of Columbus's crew on October 12, 1492, more than two months after they had set off from Spain. The land found was one of the islands of the modern Bahamas. Columbus named it San Salvador. The local population were called Arawaks, but Columbus was convinced that he had arrived at the Indies, so he called them Indians.

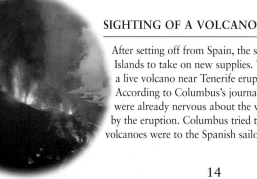

SIGHTING OF A VOLCANO

After setting off from Spain, the ships landed at the Canary Islands to take on new supplies. While he was there, a live volcano near Tenerife erupted on August 24, 1492. According to Columbus's journal, many of the crew, who were already nervous about the voyage, were frightened by the eruption. Columbus tried to explain what volcanoes were to the Spanish sailors.

THE SHIPS
ON THE VOYAGE

Columbus took three ships on his journey across the Atlantic Ocean. They were the Pinta, the Niña (captained by Pinzon and his brother), and Columbus's own ship the *Santa Maria*. The *Santa Maria* was just over 100 ft. long (55m), with the others just half that length. The total crew for these three ships numbered 90 men.

RETURN TO SPAIN

When Columbus left Hispaniola, he left 38 men behind and enough food and ammunition for a year. He and his crew moved on to the *Niña* and set off for Spain on January 4, 1493. The *Pinta* joined the *Niña* on January 6. Eventually, he arrived at the Azores on February 18, and Portugal on March 4. Columbus then sailed to Palos on March 15 and went to meet the king and queen in Barcelona in triumph.

CUBA AND ONWARDS

After leaving San Salvador, Columbus arrived in Cuba. He was convinced that he had arrived in China and sent off a team to find the "Great Khan." They came back after finding nothing. The ships then sailed to Haiti, which Columbus named Hispaniola (the "Spanish Island"). According to the first published account of the people of the New World, in 1497, they lived to 150, had no government, and ate human flesh.

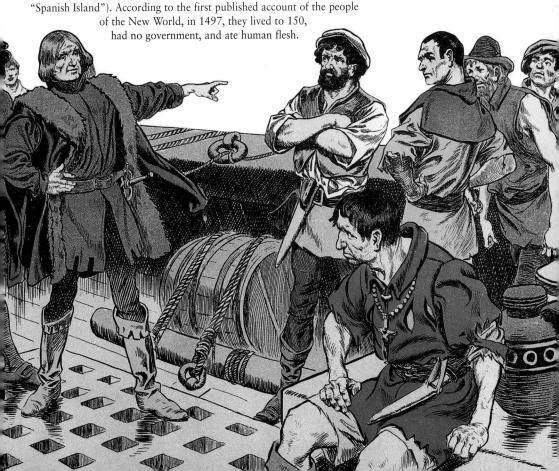

A NEW CONTINENT

During Columbus's later voyages, it became clear that he had not found a new route to the Indies. Instead, he had discovered a continent unknown to the Europeans. After meeting natives in Venezuela on his third journey, in 1498, he wrote in his journal that he had found "A very great continent . . . where Christianity will have so much enjoyment and our faith in time so great an increase."

SHIPS FOR LATER VOYAGES

While Columbus had only three ships on his first voyage, things were very different for his second. Ferdinand and Isabella were so eager for Spain to stay in control of what they thought was the westward route to Asia that they gave Columbus 17 ships. The fact that his third voyage had only six ships, and his fourth voyage had just four, shows how much Columbus fell from favor with Ferdinand and Isabella.

CHRISTOPHER COLUMBUS -A TIMELINE-

~1488~

The Cape of Good Hope reached by Bartolomeu Diaz

~1490~

The commission under Talavera recommends that the Spanish royal family turn down Columbus's proposals

~1492~

Christopher Columbus sets off on his first voyage and lands at San Salvador

~1493~

Christopher Columbus returns to Spain and sets off on his second voyage

THE DISCOVERY OF VENEZUELA

Columbus set off on his third voyage on May 30, 1498. He was searching for the mainland that he believed should have been near the islands that he had discovered. After discovering the island of Trinidad in July 1498, he sailed to the coast of South America. On August 5, 1498, he landed on the coast of Venezuela and became the first European to set foot in South America. He also sighted the Orinoco River, which runs between Venezuela and Brazil. Columbus believed that Venezuela was part of an island and that Cuba was part of the mainland.

COLUMBUS'S LATER VOYAGES . . .

When Columbus arrived at the royal court in Barcelona, he was received by Ferdinand and Isabella with a great deal of honor. Columbus had brought back some gold, amber, and an escort of "Indians." Both monarchs were convinced that Columbus had reached the Indies. He was made Governor of

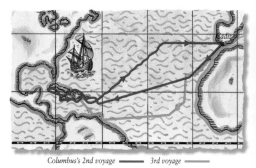

the Indies and Admiral of the Ocean Sea. He was urged to go on another expedition as soon as possible to explore and colonize the lands. Ferdinand and Isabella were concerned that the

Columbus's 2nd voyage ——— *3rd voyage* ———

Portuguese would send their own ships and claim the land as theirs, so Columbus went on another three journeys across the Atlantic Ocean, but none of them proved as successful as the first.

SHIPWRECKED OFF JAMAICA

His fourth and last voyage in 1502 was perhaps his most difficult. He had to pay for the voyage himself. After dealing with a mutiny from his crew, a storm almost destroyed his ships, and he was shipwrecked on Jamaica for a year.

COLUMBUS AS GOVERNOR

On his second voyage, Columbus returned to Navidad and found that the entire camp had been destroyed and the Spaniards killed. He ordered that a new colony called Isabela be built. In April 1494, he left to explore Cuba and Jamaica and returned to Isabela five months later as governor of the Indies. He was not a good governor. He argued with the Spanish nobles and administrators sent by Ferdinand and Isabella. He returned to Spain in June 1496 with none of the riches that he had promised the two monarchs.

... COLUMBUS'S LATER VOYAGES

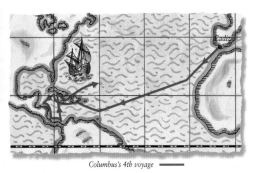

Columbus's 4th voyage ━━━

Columbus gradually fell from favor at the Spanish court, as his subsequent voyages proved less successful than the first. The king and queen remained loyal to him, but they realized that, while he was a great explorer, he was not competent as a governor. During his third voyage in 1498, he found that the colonists left behind from a previous trip were fighting among themselves. The two monarchs sent Francisco de Bobadilla to take over the governorship from Columbus. Columbus regarded this decision as a betrayal. He was arrested and sent back to Spain in 1500. On his arrival at court, Ferdinand and Isabella ordered his release. He was treated with respect, but they refused to make him governor of the "Indies" again. The French and the English were beginning to explore this New World, and Spain needed somebody capable to look after their interests there.

THE NEED FOR GOLD

The lack of gold brought back from Columbus's expeditions proved to be his downfall. He failed to convince his royal supporters that he had indeed discovered a new route to Asia. His later voyages were also marred by ill-disciplined and gold-hungry crews.

VISITING THE MAINLAND

Columbus rarely visited the mainland of the American continent. It was only on his third voyage that he eventually landed in Venezuela in South America. On his fourth voyage, he explored the coast of Central America. He visited the Gulf of Mexico and the coasts of Honduras, Nicaragua, Costa Rica (shown here), and Panama. He was still looking for a sea route to the Indies.

THE DEATH OF COLUMBUS

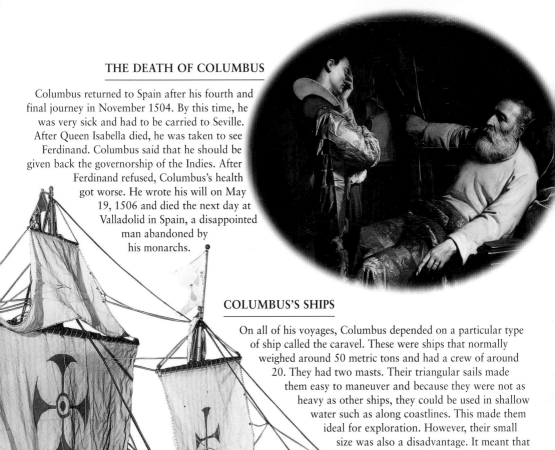

Columbus returned to Spain after his fourth and final journey in November 1504. By this time, he was very sick and had to be carried to Seville. After Queen Isabella died, he was taken to see Ferdinand. Columbus said that he should be given back the governorship of the Indies. After Ferdinand refused, Columbus's health got worse. He wrote his will on May 19, 1506 and died the next day at Valladolid in Spain, a disappointed man abandoned by his monarchs.

COLUMBUS'S SHIPS

On all of his voyages, Columbus depended on a particular type of ship called the caravel. These were ships that normally weighed around 50 metric tons and had a crew of around 20. They had two masts. Their triangular sails made them easy to maneuver and because they were not as heavy as other ships, they could be used in shallow water such as along coastlines. This made them ideal for exploration. However, their small size was also a disadvantage. It meant that they could only carry limited amounts of food, water, and other supplies. On long journeys, an ever-present problem arose over the ability to carry sufficient food and water for the duration of the voyage. Gradually, explorers began to use larger vessels called "carracks" to carry their provisions.

DIEGO COLUMBUS

Several members of the Columbus family took part in the early voyages. Columbus's brother, Bartolomé, was in charge of the colony of Isabela during his second voyage. Columbus's eldest son, Diego (on the left of the picture), served as a page to Prince Juan, heir to the two thrones of Spain. When Columbus died, Diego was named as Admiral of the Indies and governor of Hispaniola. He continued to claim all of the privileges that Ferdinand and Isabella first gave to his father. He was not successful.

SHIPS & SAILING

The crews of the early voyages of exploration faced many dangers. Not only did they have to put up with cramped conditions and only a small supply of food and water (which was often bad), but they were sailing into the unknown with little idea where they were and how fast they were traveling. Perhaps it is not surprising, therefore, that Columbus and others often had to face mutiny. Today, ships have little trouble locating their exact position. Accurate maps, clocks, and global positioning satellites (GPS) mean that sailors can tell where they are to within a few feet. Sailors in the 1400s and 1500s were not so fortunate.

MAGNETIC COMPASS

It was vitally important that the sailors crossing the Atlantic Ocean knew exactly what direction they were sailing in. On a clear day or night, either the Sun or the North Star were used. They could also use a magnetic compass. The magnetic field around Earth meant that a magnetized needle floating in water would always point northward.

DEAD RECKONING

If a navigator knew where his ship sailed from, what its speed was, the direction the ship was traveling in, and how long they had been traveling, then it was possible to calculate how far they had traveled by "dead-reckoning" and so find their position. However, winds and tides meant that this was only an approximate way of figuring out the ships position. Columbus was regarded as a great navigator because of his skill with "dead-reckoning."

THE ASTROLABE

Every navigator in Columbus's time made use of the astrolabe (similar to this Arabic example). It could be used to find out how far north or south of the equator (latitude) the ship was. It worked by measuring the height of the North Star or noon Sun from the ship. Once the height was known, then the navigator could calculate how far north or south he was.

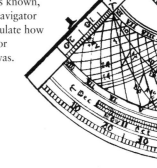

THE CROSS-STAFF

The simplest way to measure the latitude of a ship was to use an instrument called a cross-staff. It had a crossbar for sighting and a rod with measurements cut into the side. The crossbar would be lined up between the Sun or North Star and the horizon. The measurements of the long piece of wood would then tell the navigator the angle of the Sun or star from the horizon. From this, he could figure out his latitude. There is considerable danger in staring at the sun for too long. In 1595, Captain John Davis invented the back-staff, which used mirrors and shadows so that navigators did not risk being injured.

TELLING THE TIME

For the navigator to calculate a ship's position, it was vital that he knew what time of day it was. Sailors would be given the job of watching a large sand-filled hourglass (similar to this 17th-century example, shown here). It normally emptied after 30 minutes and then a bell would be rung so that everybody on board knew what the time was.

THE QUADRANT

Alongside the astrolabe, it is likely that Columbus took some quadrants with him. When Ferdinand Magellan started on his famous voyage around the world in 1519, he took seven astrolabes and 21 quadrants. Quadrants did basically the same job as astrolabes. They worked by lining up one arm with the horizon and then moving a movable arm so that it was pointing at either the Sun or North Star. The angle between these two arms could then be used to calculate the ship's latitude. It could only really work when the sea was calm and still.

Navigation

In these days of radar, computer technology, and satellites, it is easy to underestimate the great navigational skills of the early seafarers. For the large part they were sailing uncharted seas and had to estimate their position as best they could, using only the positions of heavenly bodies to guide them. Until the development of more refined instruments, such as the chronometer in the mid-18th century, navigation was a very inexact science and relied heavily on the observational skills of the individual. Needless to say, there were many accidents, particularly if the ships were blown off-course by bad weather into unknown waters.

GUIDED BY THE STARS

During the late 15th and 16th centuries the cross-staff became commonly used to calculate a ship's latitude (north-south position) at night. It comprised two pieces of wood, similar in appearance to a crossbow, with graduated scales marked along the length. By observing the angle between the horizon and the North (or Pole) Star and taking a reading off the scale, coupled with a compass reading, the ship's approximate position could be calculated. Shown here is a buckstaff, invented about 1594, for measuring the height of the sun for the same purpose.

THE "MARINER'S MIRROUR"

Following Magellan's, and later Drake's, circumnavigation of the world, it became possible to more accurately assess the Earth's size, which led in turn to the production of more accurate charts. The first sea atlas to be published in England, in 1588, was the *Mariner's Mirrour*. It was a collection of maps and charts showing the known coastlines of the world, derived from Dutch originals. The Dutch were at that time an English ally against Spain and at the forefront of navigational techniques.

LODESTONE

One of the main problems facing Elizabethan navigators was accurately calculating a ship's longitude (east-west position). Here, the astronomer-mathematician Flavius tries to do so by floating a piece of lodestone (a form of iron oxide) in a bowl of water, whilst making calculations.

STEERING BY THE SUN

This view shows an Elizabethan navigator trying to calculate the ship's latitude by use of a compass and an early form of quadrant to measure the angle of the sun's rays. However, precise timekeeping was necessary to ensure the accuracy of the calculations so at best a ship's position could only be approximated. The first fully successful sea-clock (chronometer) was not developed until 1759.

DRAKE'S DIAL

By Elizabethan times, compasses and other astronomical instruments had become quite sophisticated, as can be seen in this beautifully crafted astronomical compendium. It was made of brass in 1569 by Humphrey Cole, one of the finest scientific instrument makers of the time, and was once believed to have belonged to Francis Drake. The compendium comprised a compass, along with lunar and solar dials which, as well as being an astronomical aid, enabled the user to calculate the time. Engraved on the casing were the latitudes of many important ports around the world.

NAVIGATION -A TIMELINE-

~1588~

The first sea atlas, the "Mariner's Mirrour" is published in England

~1594~

The buckstaff is invented. It measures the height of the sun

~1759~

The first successful sea chronometer is produced

GETTING YOUR BEARINGS

The ancient Chinese discovered that lodestone is naturally magnetic and if suspended on a string will always point to the north. Early navigators made good use of this natural material but it was somewhat crude. Sometime in the 12th century, European navigators discovered that a needle could be similarly magnetized by stroking it with a lodestone. This discovery eventually led to the development of more sophisticated and accurate compasses, with the needle balanced on a central pivot. The example shown here is encased in an ivory bowl and dates from about 1580.

LIFE ON BOARD

Life on board ship in Elizabethan times was extremely harsh and the pay (which was frequently in arrears) was very poor. But, faced with abject poverty on land at a time when many country people were being forcibly ejected from their land because of changing farming practices, many had little option. A fair proportion of a ship's crew would also have been criminals escaping justice, which often led to problems with discipline. The mortality rate amongst an average crew was very high and it would be considered normal for a ship to return to port with only a quarter of the men left alive. To ensure they had enough men left to make the return journey most captains oversubscribed when signing on a new crew, but this in itself led to problems of overcrowding and food rationing. Conditions on board were cramped, each man usually sleeping in a hammock slung below decks at his place of work. Toilet facilities were virtually non-existent.

JACK-OF-ALL-TRADES

A crew on a 15th century ship had to be completely self-sufficient, for they were often away at sea for several years and might go many months between landings. As well as being able to handle the ship, sailors had to master other essential skills, such as carpentry, sailmaking, ropemaking, and cooking.

DISEASE

The most common form of disease encountered aboard ship was scurvy, a deficiency of vitamin C, caused by lack of fresh fruit and vegetables. The symptoms include bleeding into the skin and teeth loosening. Resistance to infection is also lowered, often resulting in death if untreated. All ships carried their share of rats, which might spread infectious diseases such as plague. Other common diseases were malaria, typhoid, and dysentery.

DRUNKENNESS

One of the common problems facing any captain commanding an early explorer's ship on a long voyage was boredom and the unruly behavior of his crew. With fresh water in short supply, the only drink available was beer (a gallon per crew member per day) or other stronger alcohols, which frequently led to drunkenness, not only on board but in port. Discipline was therefore very harsh to avoid potentially fatal accidents at sea.

THE CHATHAM CHEST

After the Armada of 1588, so
many seamen were wounded and
maimed that Sir John Hawkins
established the "Chatham Chest"—
the first seamen's charity. All sailors
in the Navy had to pay six pence
a month from their wages into
it for welfare purposes. This is
the chest of 1625.

THE ART OF THE GUNNER

Most 15th century ships carried a number
of cannon (a mortar is shown here), usually
made from cast iron or bronze. They were
mounted on carriages and secured in place
by heavy ropes to control the recoil when
being fired and to prevent them coming
adrift in heavy seas. They were used mostly
to disable a ship before boarding.

HEALTH & SAFETY

The health and safety of the crew aboard a typical 15th century ship was,
to say the least, extremely hazardous. There were many accidents
in simply carrying out the day-to-day tasks of sailing. Injuries
sustained during encounters with enemy vessels, usually at
close quarters, were horrific. Most ships carried a surgeon,
but the treatment he was able to administer was both
limited and very crude. By far the most common
form of treatment was the amputation of badly
damaged or infected limbs. There was no
anesthetic (other than to make the
patient drunk) and the survival rate
was appallingly low. Many of those
who survived surgery died from
gangrene afterward.

DAILY SUSTENANCE

All of the ship's food was prepared in the
galley and then distributed among the crew.
Food was rarely fresh and might consist of
biscuit, salted beef, or fish, supplemented by
cheese and gruel, a kind of porridge mix. Drinking
water was usually scarce but most ships carried a
plentiful supply of beer. The pieces of tableware
shown here were retrieved from Henry VIII's ship
the *Mary Rose* and are typical of items in
use throughout the Tudor period.

JOHN CABOT

Henry VII of England heard of Columbus's discoveries and approached John Cabot, who claimed that he could reach Asia across the North Atlantic Ocean. On his first voyage in 1497, he reached Canada and returned to a hero's welcome. However, Cabot and all of his crew disappeared without a trace during their second voyage in 1498.

THE NORTHWEST PASSAGE

Once it was realized that this land was not Asia but a new continent, explorers wanted to find a way around it. Ferdinand Magellan found a way around the southern tip of America, so the French and English looked for a route through northern waters.

CHRISTOPHER COLUMBUS
-A TIMELINE-

~1494~

Treaty of Tordesillas between Spain and Portugal signed, dividing the non-Christian world between them

~1497~

Vasco da Gama sets sail for the Indies

John Cabot sets sail from England to find a new route to Asia

Columbus begins his third voyage

~1498~

Vasco da Gama arrives in India

THE INUIT

The natives that Frobisher met in Canada called themselves Inuit. This translates into English as "people." Those who lived south of the Inuit called them Eskimos, which means "eaters of raw meat." Frobisher regarded them as savages, but they had devised a way of living in one of the harshest places known.

SAILING INTO DANGER

Explorers searching for the Northwest Passage soon discovered the dangers of such a voyage. The farther north they went, the colder the climate became. Rope and sails would freeze, and there was the constant danger of icebergs or being stuck fast in an ice sheet.

FIGHTING THE INUIT

Frobisher's crew fought with the Inuit, who had kidnapped five of his crew. He decided to capture an Inuit in a kayak. He drew him to his ship by ringing a bell over the side and then suddenly grabbing him. On his return to England, both the unfortunate Inuit and his kayak were presented to the king.

VOYAGES TO NORTH AMERICA . . .

One of the reasons why Ferdinand and Isabella were not keen to allow Christopher Columbus to remain as governor of the newly discovered lands was the threat from other European powers, especially France and England. The Spanish believed that the French and English would try to take the land away for themselves, so they sent ships and weapons and set up colonies with strong governors. It worked too well. The French and English explorers simply ignored the parts of America that the Spanish had

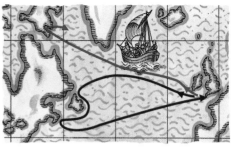

Frobisher ━━━ Cabot ━━━

conquered. It would have been too expensive in terms of money and lives to attempt to overthrow them. Instead, they turned their attention to the unexplored lands of North America and Canada, embarking on a series of ventures which soon enabled them to gain a strong foothold in the New World for themselves.

SIR MARTIN FROBISHER

This picture shows Sir Martin Frobisher's crew fighting with the Inuit in Canada. Frobisher had sailed to Canada to try and discover the Northwest Passage to Asia. He set off from London, England in June 1576 with three ships. One ship sank off Greenland, and another turned back after the crew mutinied. Frobisher sailed on and reached Baffin Island. He, too, thought, mistakenly, that he had found the route through to Asia.

. . . Voyages to North America

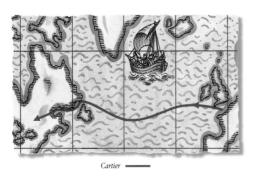

Cartier ———

The Spanish and Portuguese soon realized that the lands they had discovered were not the Indies and that it would be very difficult to sail around South America to Asia. They began to look for any wealth that they could find in their new lands. French and English explorers also started to search for riches in North America and Canada. Like the Spaniards and Portuguese, they were looking for gold. The French explorer Jacques Cartier sailed along the coast of Canada, searching for the Northwest Passage. He abandoned this search when local people, the Hurons, told him of land to the west full of gold and rubies. He set off inland but his search was unsuccessful.

TRADING IN FUR

The French exploration of Canada became dominated by the fur trade from animals such as beaver and elk. The native Canadians were essential to this trade as trackers and guides. In return, they were given alcohol and guns, which they used to fight among themselves. The English explorers were less interested in the fur trade and instead began to start exploiting the oceans surrounding Canada. John Cabot reported that he found schools of fish so big that they slowed down his ship. Canadian fish became a common food in England.

FOOL'S GOLD

When Sir Martin Frobisher arrived at Baffin Island, he found pieces of black rock that he thought might be gold. He returned in 1577 and collected 200 metric tons. A year later, he went on a third trip, taking 30 tin miners from Cornwall with him. With the backing of rich investors, he took 15 ships on the voyage. Frobisher came home with 1,000 metric tons of the rock, but what he had found was iron pyrite, known as "fool's gold." Frobisher was ruined, and the investors lost all their money.

COLONIZATION

Like the Spanish and the Portuguese, the English and French authorities began to realize that they could only really hold on to the land they had discovered by establishing colonies. These new colonies depended on the trade created by the explorers. Early French settlements, like Port Royal in Nova Scotia and Quebec, were based entirely on the fur trade. The English built settlements in Newfoundland in order to salt and pack cod destined for English tables.

FINDING THE NORTHWEST PASSAGE

Terrible sailing conditions were not the only reason why several English and French explorers were discouraged in their quest to find the Northwest Passage. On several occasions, they sailed into large inlets, which they thought were a way through to the Pacific Ocean and Asia; only Jacques Cartier sailed into the mouth of the Saint Lawrence River and thought that he had found a route through America. So did Sir Martin Frobisher in 1576, when he sailed on alone and discovered Frobisher Bay on Baffin Island. The Northwest Passage was not successfully negotiated until 1903.

CHRISTOPHER COLUMBUS
-A TIMELINE-

~1498~

John Cabot sets off on his second voyage

~1499~

Vasco da Gama returns to Portugal

~1500~

Brazil discovered by Pedro Cabral

Columbus arrested and sent back to Spain

~1502~

Vasco makes a second voyage to India to avenge the massacre of Portuguese in Calicut

Lisbon

Diaz ⎯⎯

THE EXPLORATION OF AFRICA . . .

Portugal and Spain had been conquered by the Moors in the 600s. Portugal finally threw out the Islamic invaders in 1249, and King John I of Portugal went on to conquer part of Morocco. Portugal's position on the Atlantic coastline made it ideally placed for overseas exploration, and Portuguese mariners began to look for a way to the Indies around Africa. By 1419, they had reached Madeira, and in 1431 they sailed to the Azores. In 1445, Portuguese sailors had gone around Cape Verde, the western tip of West Africa. By 1482, they had crossed the equator and reached the mouth of the Congo River.

ENCOUNTERS WITH AFRICANS

When the Portuguese sailors came into contact with the peoples who lived in Africa, they must have been amazed by their culture and appearance. Sculptures like this brass figure made by a member of the Asante people, who came from modern-day Ghana, would have looked very strange indeed. The Africans must also have been astonished by the Portuguese sailors when they first appeared off the coast in their tall ships.

PRINCE HENRY THE NAVIGATOR

Prince Henry the Navigator was the third son of John I. He spent his life studying navigation and directed the Portuguese exploration of the west African coast. He was a devout Christian who wanted to launch a crusade to drive the Muslims out of north Africa. Finding a way to Asia would help pay for this crusade and at the same time would weaken the hold that the Muslims had over the trade in gold and spices between Europe and Asia.

THE LEGEND OF PRESTER JOHN

One of the ways that Henry the Navigator hoped to destroy Muslim North Africa was to find Prester John. From the crusades onward, there were stories in Europe of a legendary Christian king named Prester John who ruled a kingdom somewhere in Africa. There were other stories that placed his kingdom in south Asia.

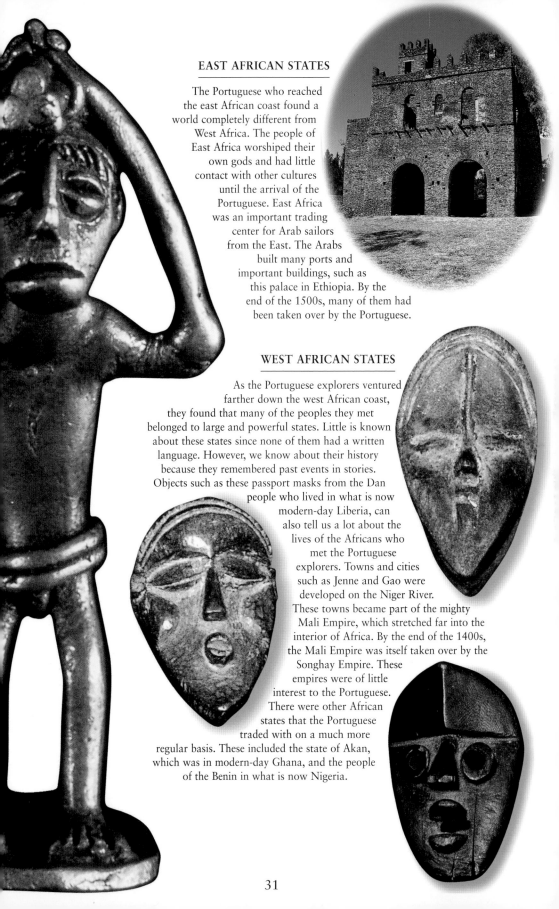

EAST AFRICAN STATES

The Portuguese who reached the east African coast found a world completely different from West Africa. The people of East Africa worshiped their own gods and had little contact with other cultures until the arrival of the Portuguese. East Africa was an important trading center for Arab sailors from the East. The Arabs built many ports and important buildings, such as this palace in Ethiopia. By the end of the 1500s, many of them had been taken over by the Portuguese.

WEST AFRICAN STATES

As the Portuguese explorers ventured farther down the west African coast, they found that many of the peoples they met belonged to large and powerful states. Little is known about these states since none of them had a written language. However, we know about their history because they remembered past events in stories. Objects such as these passport masks from the Dan people who lived in what is now modern-day Liberia, can also tell us a lot about the lives of the Africans who met the Portuguese explorers. Towns and cities such as Jenne and Gao were developed on the Niger River. These towns became part of the mighty Mali Empire, which stretched far into the interior of Africa. By the end of the 1400s, the Mali Empire was itself taken over by the Songhay Empire. These empires were of little interest to the Portuguese. There were other African states that the Portuguese traded with on a much more regular basis. These included the state of Akan, which was in modern-day Ghana, and the people of the Benin in what is now Nigeria.

... THE EXPLORATION OF AFRICA

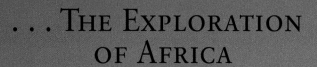

The Portuguese were not interested in exploring the interior of Africa. They did trade with the peoples that they encountered, but they were looking for a sea route to the Indies. However, they knew that places on the coast of Africa were important landing stages for ships. The route around Africa to Asia took many years to discover. In 1482, King John II sent Diogo Cao to find the Indies. He did not find it, but he did discover that Africa was much larger than many people thought. It was Bartolomeu Diaz in 1488 who finally sailed around the southern tip of Africa. He followed the coast of Africa and sailed farther south than any other European had managed until then.

BARTOLOMEU DIAZ

Diaz's ships were driven out of sight of land by a fierce storm. When it became calm, he sailed north and found that the coast was now on his left and not his right, as expected. He had sailed around the southern tip of Africa by accident.

TRADING WITH AFRICANS

The two things that the Portuguese wanted when trading with the Akan and Benin peoples were gold and slaves. The Akan supplied most of West Africa's gold, which came from rivers in the interior of Africa. The Portuguese bought this gold from the Akan with slaves that they had either captured themselves or bought from the Benin people. Many slaves were also transported back to Portugal and sold again.

BUILDING IN AFRICA

The Portuguese did not explore the interior of Africa, and they decided not to establish any African colonies at this stage. However, they knew they had to protect their trade routes to Asia so they built a series of forts along the coastline. They could supply and protect Portuguese ships and keep out foreign competitors.

THE CAPE OF GOOD HOPE

When Bartolomeu Diaz reached the southern tip of Africa, he decided to call it "Cabo Tormentoso," which means the Cape of Storms. King John II rejected this name because it was too gloomy and gave it the name "Cape of Good Hope", because it raised hopes of eventually reaching the Indies.

~1502~

*Columbus sets off on his
fourth and final voyage*

~1506~

*Columbus dies at
Valladolid*

~1509~

*The Arab fleet is destroyed
by the Portuguese at the
battle of Diu*

~1510~

*Alfonso de Albuquerque
captures Goa*

~1511~

*Alfonso de Albuquerque
captures Malacca*

~1513~

*The Portuguese
reach China*

~1524~

*Vasco da Gama appointed
Viceroy of India*

*Vasco da Gama dies and is
buried at Cochin in India*

~1530~

*The Portuguese establish
trading bases in Bombay
and Sri Lanka*

THE RICHES OF
THE INDIES

Bartolomeu Diaz was given the task of preparing da Gama's ships for the journey. He loaded them with objects to trade with the Africans, such as hawkbells, rings, cloth, and olive oil. It did not occur to him that the rulers of the Indies would not be impressed with these objects. The picture shows how wealthy and abundant in food the Indies were. This cargo was to cause da Gama some problems when he arrived in India.

DA GAMA'S SHIPS

Da Gama had a fleet of four ships: the *San Gabriel*, the *Sao Rafael*, the *Barrio*, and a storage ship that had no name but had a three-year supply of food and drink. The ships set off from Lisbon on July 8, 1497. The picture shows the storeship burning. This was done deliberately by da Gama because he was afraid that if the storeship was lost in bad weather, then his crew would starve. The supplies were crammed on to the other ships before the empty storeship was set alight.

CLAIMING LAND FOR PORTUGAL

Among the stores that da Gama carried on his voyage were stone crosses called padroes. These were set in high ground to act as markers for crews who were to follow them. They were also used when Portugal claimed any newly discovered land. This cross is at Malindi in modern-day Kenya. Da Gama had a difficult time in East Africa because Arab traders did not welcome them there.

INDIA & THE INDIAN OCEAN . . .

The Portuguese did more than build forts to protect their trade routes to the Indies. In 1494, Spain and Portugal signed the Treaty of Tordesillas, which divided the world between the two countries. It gave Spain control over all non-Christian lands west of an imaginary line in the mid-Atlantic Ocean. Portugal was given everything to the east. This meant that only the Portuguese could use the route around Africa to Asia. It took ten years after Bartolomeu Diaz had discovered the way round Africa for Portuguese ships to finally reach India. The new king of Portugal, Manuel I, chose Vasco da Gama to lead this expedition.

da Gama ———— Cabral ————

VASCO DA GAMA

Very little is known about Vasco da Gama's early life. He was born sometime in the early 1460s and became a soldier. He also studied navigation from Portuguese sailors. It was this skill, together with his military knowledge and qualities as a leader, that made him the ideal candidate for Portugal's first expedition to the Indies.

DEALING WITH MUTINY

King Manuel I had chosen da Gama because he had a reputation for being a good leader and for keeping discipline. At first da Gama had to sail out into the Atlantic Ocean to catch the wind that would take him eastward. He was out of sight of land for 13 weeks. Some of the crew thought they would never see land again. They mutinied and tried to force da Gama to return home, but he convinced them that they would land soon. The ringleaders of the mutiny were arrested and bound in chains.

. . . INDIA & THE INDIAN OCEAN

When da Gama reached the east African port of Malindi, he saw four ships that looked strange to him. This was his first contact with Indian traders. The sultan of Malindi turned out to be friendly and helped da Gama with the rest of his trip. When da Gama set off across the Indian Ocean, he had on board a pilot named Ahmed ibn Majid. With his help, da Gama managed to sail across the Indian Ocean in only 23 days. He arrived in Calicut, the main trading city in southern India, on May 20, 1498. The eastward route to Asia had been found.

BOMBARDING CALICUT

Another explorer named Pedro Cabral was sent to Calicut after da Gama had returned to Portugal. He set up a trading center in Calicut, left behind some Portuguese traders, and sailed home. Local Muslims attacked the center and killed everybody inside. Da Gama was sent to take revenge. When he reached Calicut in 1502, he bombarded the city with cannon. From then on, the Portuguese controlled the Indian trade routes with military force.

HINDUS OR CHRISTIANS?

Until da Gama reached India, no European had even heard of Hinduism, the main religion of India. When da Gama first saw a Hindu temple, he was convinced that the people must be Christians. He thought a statue of a goddess, like the one shown, was the Virgin Mary. Images of gods and goddesses painted on the wall seemed to be Christian saints. Da Gama returned to Portugal with tales of Indian Christians.

RETURN TO PORTUGAL

The picture shows the king of Portugal, Manuel I, greeting da Gama on his return from India. Da Gama had set off from Calicut on August 29, 1498. He decided to avoid East Africa. Such a long voyage without taking on fresh supplies had a terrible effect on the crew. When he reached Lisbon in September 1499, only 54 out of the original crew of 170 were still alive. King Manuel was overjoyed. Portugal had beaten Spain in the race to reach the Indies.

BUILDING AN EMPIRE

From centers such as Goa and the rebuilt city of Calicut, shown here, the Portuguese began to take control of the rest of the Asian trade routes. They reached China in 1513 and Japan in 1542. The Portuguese knew that many of the spices they found in India came from some islands in Southeast Asia. They decided that they had to control the route to these islands. In 1511, Alfonso de Albuquerque captured the Muslim port of Malacca, controlled this route. From Malacca, the Portuguese could easily reach the islands that grew spices.

FIGHTING FOR CONTROL

The Portuguese were determined to take control of trade with India. King Manuel sent two commanders, Alfonso de Albuquerque and Francisco de Almeida, to carry out this task. De Almeida sailed along the east African coast and attacked the Arab traders who had caused da Gama such difficulties. Muslim oared galleys were no match for Portuguese ships, and in the Battle of Diu the entire Muslim fleet was destroyed. Goa was captured by Alfonso de Albuquerque in 1510. He burned the city to the ground and built a new city. The picture shows a Portuguese-style building in Goa.

ARRIVAL AT CALICUT

The ruler of Calicut was called the Zamorin. When da Gama met the Zamorin he laid out the gifts he had brought with him. The Zamorin was insulted by what he saw as cheap goods and sent da Gama away. Da Gama was allowed to trade but could not compete with the Arab traders. He spent three months in Calicut but managed to buy only a few spices. After a dispute with the Zamorin over taxes, da Gama decided to sail for home.

STUCK IN THE ICE

Willem Barents was a Dutch explorer who was also trying to find a way to Asia around Russia. He made three voyages into the north. During the third voyage, his ship became stuck. He was eventually forced to abandon his ship after the ice began to crush it.

WILLOUGHBY'S FATE

As Willoughby sailed northward, a strong wind separated the three ships. Willoughby found one ship, but Chancellor's ship had disappeared. He sailed on to Lapland. The weather was getting colder, and his ships found it impossible to move as the sea began to freeze. He decided to stop for the winter. The extreme cold and scurvy claimed the lives of Willoughby and all of his crew.

SAMOYED ARCHERS

CHRISTOPHER COLUMBUS
-A TIMELINE-

~1534~

Jacques Cartier tries to find the Northwest Passage

~1542~

The Portuguese reach Japan

~1551~

English merchants form a company to fund a expedition to find the Northeast Passage

Explorers of northern Russia were surprised to find people who lived in the Arctic wastes. The Samoyed were a nomadic people who moved into the north of Russia during the summer and then, as the winter set in, south to the warmer Russian tundra. They survived by herding nomadic reindeer. It is believed that less than 30,000 Samoyedic are still alive today. "Samoyed" was actually the wrong name for these people—a mistake in Russian etymology. Nowadays, these people are known as the "Nenets."

BARENTS IN THE WINTER

When Barents and his crew had to abandon their ship, they walked across the frozen sea to the island of Novaya Zemlya. They built a shelter made from the wood of their ship and spent the winter there. They killed polar bears for their fat, which they used in their oil lamps. In the spring, they sailed back to Lapland in small lifeboats.

AROUND RUSSIA—
THE NORTHEAST PASSAGE

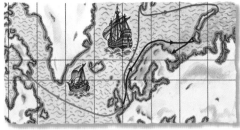

Frobisher ▬▬▬▬ Willoughby ▬▬▬▬ Barents ▬▬▬▬

It must have seemed to the English that between them, Spain and Portugal had taken over all of trade with the East. Da Gama had reached India after voyaging eastward around Africa, and Magellan had sailed to Asia from the west in 1520–1521. English and French attempts to find a passage across the top of Canada had come to nothing. It was perhaps inevitable that some would search for a route to Asia by sailing through the Arctic and across northern Russia. In late 1551, a group of English merchants formed a company to try to find a new route to Asia. Sebastian Cabot, the son of John Cabot, was made head of the company. The voyage was to be led by Sir Hugh Willoughby. Richard Chancellor was his deputy and was well known as a skilled navigator. The expedition set off on May 10, 1553 from London, England.

FACING DANGER

Explorers looking for the Northeast Passage had to face many of the problems faced by those explorers who were looking for a way to Asia around Canada. During an Arctic winter, the sea itself froze and ships could be crushed. In warmer weather, loose chunks of ice also posed a threat, as did polar bears who were also known to attack sailors.

IVAN THE TERRIBLE

When Richard Chancellor was separated from Willoughby, he continued sailing until he reached the coast of Russia. There, he was well treated and taken to Moscow to meet the Czar of Russia. He was called Ivan the Terrible because of his cruelty to his subjects. However, he treated Chancellor well and held a banquet in his honor. This meeting led to trade between England and Russia. The English exchanged guns and cloth for Russian fur and animal fat.

Renaissance & Other Explorers

The exploration of the Americas and Asia continued long after they were first encountered by Europeans. The explorers who came after Columbus and da Gama had many reasons for exploring these new-found lands. Sometimes, simply a love of adventure and danger. Many of them, though, hoped to find land and wealth and so make themselves and their monarchs rich. Others went with a missionary zeal, wanting to convert anyone they met to Christianity. Most of the explorers of North America and Canada were either English or French. The exploration of South America and the Indies was left to the Spanish and Portuguese.

AMERICUS VESPUTIUS

AMERIGO VESPUCCI

Vespucci was an Italian sailor who had a continent named after him. He claimed to have made four voyages to the New World, but only two are certain. His travel writings were very popular, and a German mapmaker named the New World map that he was making after him—"Amerigo," or America.

WILLIAM DAMPIER

Dampier was born in England in 1651. His early life at sea included a trip to Newfoundland in Canada. In 1698, he led a scientific expedition to lands to the south of Asia that had just been discovered. His voyage took him to the west coast of Australia and the islands of Indonesia.

HENRY HUDSON

Hudson tried to find the Northeast and Northwest Passages. His first voyage was in 1607, when he tried to find the Northeast Passage, but his ship was blocked by ice. During his fourth voyage in 1610 to find the Northwest Passage, he was forced to spend the winter in freezing conditions in a bay now named after him. The crew mutinied and set him adrift in a small boat. He was never heard from again.

THOMAS CAVENDISH

Thomas Cavendish was an English explorer and the third person to sail around the globe. He set off in July 1586 from Plymouth with three ships. He discovered Port Desire in Argentina before sailing through the Strait of Magellan. He attacked Spanish ships and settlements and then sailed across the Pacific Ocean. He returned to England in 1588. He died while sailing to China.

Animum fortuna sequatur

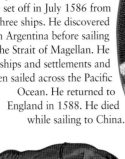

THE SHIP OF JUAN FERNANDEZ

Juan Fernandez was a Spanish navigator and explorer. In 1563, he sailed from Callao in Peru to Valparaiso in Chile, which was considered a daring feat. He went on to discover several Pacific islands in 1574. There is some evidence that he reached Australia and New Zealand in 1576.

CHRISTOPHER COLUMBUS
-A TIMELINE-

~1553~

Sir Hugh Willoughby and Richard Chancellor set off from London, England to find the Northeast Passage. Willoughby dies, and Chancellor meets Ivan the Terrible

~1569~

Spain fights a war with Portugal over the Philippines and emerges victorious

~1576~

Martin Frobisher looks for the Northwest Passage

~1577~

Frobisher begins his second voyage to search for gold

~1578~

Frobisher starts his third and last voyage in the quest for gold

~1596~

Willem Barents is trapped on Novaya Zemlya while looking for the Northeast Passage

~1608~

The French colony of Quebec in Canada founded

SAMUEL DE CHAMPLAIN

Samuel de Champlain was the son of a French naval captain. He traveled to North America and Canada 12 times between 1603–1616. From 1604–1607, he mapped much of the Canadian Atlantic coast. In 1608, he founded the tiny settlement of Quebec, which was to become the capital of French colonists in Canada. He went on to discover the Ottawa River and the lakes Champlain, Ontario, and Huron.

DID YOU KNOW?

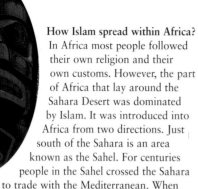

How Islam spread within Africa?
In Africa most people followed their own religion and their own customs. However, the part of Africa that lay around the Sahara Desert was dominated by Islam. It was introduced into Africa from two directions. Just south of the Sahara is an area known as the Sahel. For centuries people in the Sahel crossed the Sahara to trade with the Mediterranean. When Islam spread across North Africa in the seventh and eighth centuries, Islam found its way across the desert with the traders. On the east African coast Islam arrived with Arab merchants who sailed down much of the east African coastline.

What was the first European colony in Asia?
Goa was the first European colony to be established on the Asian continent and it became the Portuguese capital in India. It was also the last part of India to become independent. India achieved independence from Britain in 1947 but Goa was not returned to India until 1961.

Why the English and the Dutch ignored the Treaty of Tordesillas?
These two countries sent out expeditions and often crossed into areas which, according to the Treaty, belonged to either Spain or Portugal. They could ignore this because the Treaty was put together by Pope Alexander VI for these two Catholic countries. Since the Netherlands and later England were Protestant they claimed that the Treaty did not apply to them.

How much the European explorers were involved in slavery?
From the 1440s the Portuguese used their expeditions along the west African coast to capture people and to take them back to Portugal to sell as slaves. Europeans felt that slavery was justified because the people they had captured were not Christians. Once they became slaves then they could become Christians. Africans began to fight back once they realized why the Europeans were there. Portuguese traders soon realized that it would be easier to buy slaves from traders in the Benin.

Where Columbus is buried?
Columbus died on May 20, 1506 at his home in Valladolid in Spain. In 1513 his body was moved to a monastery in Seville. In 1542 Columbus's remains crossed the Atlantic Ocean to Hispaniola and he was buried at the cathedral of Santa Maria in Santo Domingo. However, it is also claimed that Columbus's body lies in Havana or the cathedral of Seville.

How the Portuguese discovered Brazil?
When Vasco da Gama returned to Portugal from the Indies, Pedro Cabral set off from Lisbon with a fleet of thirteen ships in March 1500. Like da Gama, he began by sailing westward. However, he went much further than he intended. On April 22, he sighted the coast of Brazil. After claiming the land for Portugal he set off eastward for the Indies.

What ships did the Europeans use as trading vessels?
In the first part of the 16th century the carrack became the most popular European ship for trade, exploration and warfare. Carracks became important symbols of national pride. In England, Henry VIII had built the Great Harry, which was the largest carrack built up until that time. The French responded by building La Grande Françoise which was even larger. Sadly, it was so large that it could not get out of the mouth of the harbor where it was built. By the end of the 16th century the carrack was being replaced by the galleon.

Who made up a ship's crew?
Most ships not only had ordinary sailors amongst the crew but also carpenters, priests, cooks, doctors, gunners, blacksmiths, pilots, and boys as young as 10 on board. Crew members normally came from many different countries and the captain sometimes had difficulty making them understand his instructions.

What was the biggest problem faced by sailors?
The main problem faced by sailors on long voyages was scurvy. This often fatal disease is caused by a lack of vitamin C which comes from fresh fruit and vegetables. Fresh food did not last long on the ships of the explorers. Sailors would become extremely tired and would start to bleed from the scalp and the gums. However, it was not until 1915 that vitamins were identified. Citrus fruit juice

(ascorbic acid) was adopted against scurvy by the Admiralty in 1795 but before that fresh air, dry clothing, warmth, and exercise were also thought to help prevent it. There was thus much confusion about its exact cause.

Where does the term "a square meal" come from?

It is not known when this term first came into use but since at least Tudor times meals on board ship were dished up on square platters, which seamen balanced on their laps. They had frames around the edge to prevent the food from falling off and were so shaped to enable them to be easily stored when not in use. Each sailor thus received his full ration, or square meal, for the day.

How does time give longitude?

Each day (24 hours) the Earth turns through 360°, from west to east; that is, it turns through 15° of longitude every hour and 1° every 4 minutes. A place that has a 4-minute difference in time at noon from a starting point (or prime meridian) to east or west—noon in each spot being when the Sun is exactly overhead – is 1° of longitude away. Thus, accurate east/west time variations between places can be converted into relative distances and positions of longitude.

Do we still use the stars for navigation?

It is easy to assume that because navigational techniques used in the past were relatively simple they were also inaccurate. This is not necessarily true, although results need to be accurately recorded and verified to be usable. In 1967 astronomers discovered pulsars, rapidly rotating condensed stars (formed from dead stars) that emit radio waves, or pulses, as detectable beams. They pulsate at fixed rates making it possible for future space programs to utilize them for navigational purposes in outer space.

How did the Spice Islands get their name?

One of the main attractions for the Elizabethan explorers searching for new trade routes were spices from the East. The groups of islands that make up the East Indies (which include the Moluccas, Philippines, and Melanesia groups of islands) were particularly rich in such commodities and came to be known collectively as the Spice Islands.

How did America get its name?

America was named after the 16th-century navigator and mapmaker Amerigo Vespucci. Of Italian birth, in 1508 he was created Chief Royal Pilot of Spain. All Spanish captains had to provide him with full details each time they undertook a new voyage so that he could constantly amend and update his collection of sea charts. He made several voyages to the New World himself (notably in 1499–1500) and was once credited with discovering America. Although this was not true, he was the first to consider it to be an independent continent and not part of Asia. It was afterward known as "Amerigo's Land" in honor of him.

What is the history of the ancient civilizations before the explorers "discovered" them?

We know very little about the lives of the Aztecs and Incas because the Spaniards destroyed everything that they found. Beautiful gold objects were melted down into gold bars. Books and drawings were burnt as works of the devil. Bishop Diego de Landa Calderón of Yucatán came across some painted books and he wrote later: "We found a great number of books in these letters of theirs, and because they had nothing but superstition and lies of the devil, we burned them all, which upset the Indians greatly, and caused them much pain." Most of the remains of Tenochtitlan were not discovered until the Mexicans began to build an underground railway system in Mexico City.

How did the Aztec calendar work?

The Aztec calendar stone worked in a very peculiar way. The calendar was made up of two wheels, one of top of the other. The small wheel had 13 numbers carved or painted on it. The large wheel had the names of 20 days on it. These were the names of animals or plants. Numbers could then be lined up with a particular named day. Only the Aztec priests could read these and tell if a day was to be lucky or unlucky. For instance, 4 Dog was a good day to be born on. Anybody born on 2 Rabbit would not do so well. 1 Ocelot was seen as a good day for traveling.

Which continent is the coldest, driest, highest, and windiest?

Antarctica. It covers an area half as large again as the U.S.A. (about 5.5 million square miles (14 million square kilometres)) and represents a tenth of the Earth's land mass. Approximately 98 per cent of Antarctica is covered by ice, up to a 1.5 miles (2.4 kilometres) thick in places. The Elizabethan explorers had searched in vain for a habitable land mass in the southern oceans, which was not finally discovered until 1820 when Edward Bransfield landed on part of the Antarctic Peninsula.

GLOSSARY

amber Fossil tree resin, *(see below)* which is usually orange-brown in color. Amber is often used in jewelry.

amputation The surgical removal of a limb or body part.

anesthetic A drug that causes temporary loss of sensation in the body.

armada A large fleet of warships.

arrears An unpaid debt that is overdue.

astronomical Relating to the study of the Universe beyond the Earth.

awning A canopy-like covering attached to the exterior of a building to provide shelter.

baptism A Christian ceremony that signifies spiritual cleansing and rebirth.

bombardment The heavy, continuous attacking of a target with artillery.

botany The scientific study of plants and vegetation.

cannibal A person who eats the flesh of other humans.

"cat boat" A large vessel often used in the coal trade. The origins of the name are a mystery, but one theory is that the name comes from coal and timber—which these boats often transported.

charter To lease or rent services and possessions; a document issued by an authority that grants an institution certain rights or privileges.

charting Navigational mapping of coastlines and seas so that sailors can find routes for purposes of trade and exploration.

circumnavigate To travel all the way around something by ship.

civil war A war between different groups in the same country.

colonization The extension of a nation's power by the establishment of settlements and by trade in foreign lands.

commission A committee set up to deal with and look at a certain issue.

dead-reckoning A way of estimating one's current position based on a known previous position, allowing for speed, distance, and direction moved.

deck A platform built on a ship. There are often numerous decks within a ship.

dissolution The process of breaking up and destroying something. The "Dissolution of the Monasteries" was a process undertaken by King Henry VIII between 1536 and 1540, which resulted in the disbanding of all monasteries, nunneries, and friaries, and the claiming of their income, wealth, and land for the king.

draught The depth to which a ship sinks in the water, measured from its keel.

dysentery An inflammatory infection of the intestines resulting in severe diarrhea. Dysentery was a major cause of death on board ship.

electrical charge Electrical energy that has been stored.

equator The imaginary line running around the center of the Earth from east to west, at an equal distance from the North and South Poles.

expulsion The act of forcing something or someone out.

Global Positioning System Satellite system that allows users to pinpoint their location.

haberdasher A person who sells small items for sewing, such as needles, buttons, and thread.

hawkbells Bells attached to the legs of a hawk by a small leather strap, just above the talons. Bells were often organized to ring with different tones, so that in a group of hawks a pleasant sound would be produced. Hawking was a popular country sport where the hawk hunted for its owner.

hulk A ship that is afloat, but is not capable of

going to sea. It often refers to a ship that has had its rigging or equipment removed.

interior The inland part of a country.

junk A Chinese sailing ship.

keel The structural main beam running down the middle of a ship, serving as the spine of the boat's structure.

kingdom A country with a king or queen at its head.

latitude The imaginary parallel lines running east to west around the Earth.

longitude The imaginary parallel lines running north to south around the Earth.

malaria A disease spread by the bite of a mosquito.

missionary A person who tries to convert native inhabitants to their own religious viewpoint. Missionaries often provide charitable services.

mortality The likelihood of death. The mortality rate is the rate of death in a certain number of people in a population.

musket A muzzle-loading smoothbore gun (without rotational grooves to guide the projectile along the barrel) mounted in and fired from the shoulder.

mutiny A rebellion by members of a ship's crew to overthrow the captain.

native A person born in a particular place or country, and living there.

observatory A building designed and equipped for looking at the stars and for watching astronomical events.

pack-ice A large collection of ice that has combined to form a single mass. Pack-ice moves with the currents of the sea.

patronage The support, encouragement, and backing (often financial) of a person or people.

piracy Stealing whilst at sea; taking ships and possessions without the instruction of a sovereign or ruler.

primitive Relating to an early stage of technical or technological progress; a person who belongs to an early stage of civilized advancement.

purser The person on board a ship who is responsible for all things financial.

putrefaction The decomposition or breakdown of a dead creature.

pyramid A building or structure with triangular sides narrowing to a peak at the top.

sheer-legs A temporary structure of two or three tied beams, that formed a support for lifting heavy weights.

Spanish Inquisition The Spanish Inquisition was set up in 1478 by Ferdinand and Isabella of Spain. Its purpose was to ensure that Catholic orthodoxy was maintained in Spain.

Spanish Main The mainland coast of the Spanish Empire around the Caribbean area.

strait A narrow sea-channel, joining two larger bodies of water.

subdue To put down or contain by force or by authority.

sugar cane A tall fibrous grass-like plant, that naturally contains high levels of sucrose, which is refined to produce sugar.

tribute The tax system employed by the Aztecs to support their state. This was paid by all the regions under their control to finance building, military, nobility, and religion.

typhoid An illness caused by eating or drinking contaminated food or water.

zealous Filled with enthusiasm and energy in favor of a cause.

zenith The point directly above a certain location.

FURTHER READING
& WEBSITES

BOOKS

Atlas of Exploration
Andrew Kerr and Francois Naude (Dorling Kindersley Publications, 2008)

Christopher Colombus (DK Discoveries)
Peter Chrisp (DK Children, 2006)

Christopher Columbus and the Discovery of the Americas (Explorers of New Lands)
Tim McNeese (Chelsea House Publications, 2005)

Christopher Colombus: Famous Explorer (Graphic Biographies Series)
Mary D. Wade (Capstone Press, 2001)

Christopher Colombus: Sailing to a New World (In the Footsteps of Explorers)
Adrianna Morganelli (Crabtree Publishing, 2005)

Christopher Columbus: The Voyage That Changed the World (Sterling Biographies)
Emma Carlson Berne (Sterling, 2008)

Christopher Columbus: To the New World (Great Explorations)
James Lincoln Collier (Benchmark Books (NY), 2006)

Colombus: Opening up the New World (Great Explorers of the World)
Stephen Feinstein (Enslow Publishers, 2009)

Explorer (Eyewitness)
Rupert Matthews (Dorling Kindersley Publications, 2003)

Explorers & Exploration
Steadwell Books and Lara Rice Bergen (Heinemann Library, 2001)

Meet Christopher Columbus
James T. de Kay (Landmark Books)

Tools of Navigation: A Kid's Guide to the History and Science of Finding Your Way (Tools of Discovery)
Rachel Dickinson (Nomad Press, 2005)

Where Do You Think You're Going, Christopher Columbus?
Jean Fritz (Putnam Juvenile, 1997)

You Are the Explorer
Nathan Aaseng (Oliver Press, 1999)
Vancouver: University of British Columbia Press, 2005

You Wouldn't Want to Sail With Christopher Columbus!: Uncharted Waters You'd Rather Not Cross (You Wouldn't Want to . . .)
Fiona MacDonald, David Antram, David Salariya (Children's Press (CT), 2004)

WEBSITES

http://academickids.com/encyclopedia/index.php/
Christopher_Columbus
An encyclopedic biography of Columbus with great cross-referencing to subjects related to his voyages.

www.bbc.co.uk/history/british/tudors/columbus_
legacy_01.shtml
This BBC site has a detailed description of the 15th-century world that Columbus lived in and the consequences of his discoveries.

www.elizabethan-era.org.uk/christopher-columbus.htm
Timeline, facts, and a history of Columbus and his voyages.

www.enchantedlearning.com/explorers/page/
c/columbus.shtml
Provides printable maps for Columbus's routes, information on Columbus, and activities to try on Columbus Day.

www.historyguide.org/earlymod/columbus.html
An extract from the 1492 journal of Columbus.

www.kidport.com/REFLIB/UsaHistory/
Explorers/Explorers.htm
Information on early explorers including Columbus.

www.kidskonnect.com/subject-index/16-history/
265-explorers.html
A gateway to sites about the different explorers.

www.nmm.ac.uk/columbus
The National Maritime Museum, London, site with a biography and details about Columbus's voyages and the ships, seafarers, and life at sea of the time.

INDEX

ACKNOWLEDGMENTS

The publishers would like to thank: Graham Rich, Peter Done, John Guy, Val Garwood, and Elizabeth Wiggans for their assistance and David Hobbs for his map of the world. Picture research by Image Select.

Picture Credits: t=top, b=bottom, c=center, l=left, r=right, OFC=outside front cover
AKG (London); 36/37cb, 37br, 36c. Ann Ronan at Image Select; 8bl, 8/9cb, 11tr, 15b, 17r, 19br, 20bl, 26tl, 38tl, 38tr, 38bl, 38/39cb, 38c, 38r, 40bl, 41t, 48. Archivo Fotografico—Spain; 12tr, 18l. Asia; 12cb, 13tr, 41c. Bridgeman/Giraudon (France); 26/27c, 27b. British Museum; 9br. Chris Fairclough/Image Select; 16cb, 28/29c, 36/37c. Fotomas Index; 12tl. Giraudon (France); 3, 8tl, 8/9c, 8cb, 9r, 10tl, 10/11, 11ct, 12c, 14/15ct, 19tr, 20/21ct, 29tr, 34c, 34tr. Image Select; 1, 9t, 9tr, 12/13cb, 15c, 21tr, 26tl, 31br, 30l, 30b, 30/31c, 33tr, 41br, 42c. Institut Amatller D'art Hispanic (Spain); 2, 16/17c, 18/19c, 32tl. Mary Evans; 1tl, 14cl, 16/17cb, 22/23ct, 23tr, 24tl, 24bl, 34/35cb, 37tl, 36bl, 39r, 40tl, 40/41c. Mary Rose Trust; 20tl. Metropolitan Museum of Art, New York/Peter Newark/The Bridgeman Art Library; OFC. National Maritime Museum; 21br, 22tl, 22/23 ct, 24/25ct, 35br. Pix; 16tl, 26tr. Planet Earth Pictures; 28bl, 32/33. Science Photo Library; 28/29c. Spectrum Colour Library; 11tl, 14bl, 15tr, 27cr, 31tr, 32/33ct. Trip/Darren Maybury; 18cb. Werner Forman Archive; 34b, 36tl.

NOTE TO READERS
The website addresses are correct at the time of publishing. However, due to the ever-changing nature of the Internet, websites and content may change. Some websites can contain links that are unsuitable for children. The publisher is not responsible for changes in content or website addresses. We advise that Internet searches should be supervised by an adult.